# Coding

## *Complete Beginners Guide*
## *To Computer Programming*
## *To Start Creating Now*

### David Cooke

# Introduction

I want to thank you and congratulate you for purchasing the book, *"Coding: Complete Beginners Guide To Computer Programming To Start Creating Now"*.

Coding or computer programming simply entails the art of writing computer programs. Computer programs are sets of instructions that tell a computer what to do to complete a specific task. To write these sets of instructions, we use a specific computer programming language.

Coding, telling a computer what to do, is fun but it is not easy. Unlike human beings, computers do not use English, Spanish, or any of our native languages. They can only understand ones (1) and zeros (0) which represent an on and off state respectively.

Computer programs can have a single line of computer code or millions of lines of code. Today, we have many programming languages meant to help us create desktop applications, mobile applications, websites and more.

In this guide, we shall be looking at the basic essentials you need to learn to start programming or writing computer code or programs.

Thanks again for purchasing this book, I hope you enjoy it!

This document is geared towards providing exact and reliable information in regards to the topic and issue covered. The publication is sold with the idea that the publisher is not required to render accounting, officially permitted, or otherwise, qualified services. If advice is necessary, legal or professional, a practiced individual in the profession should be ordered.

- From a Declaration of Principles which was accepted and approved equally by a Committee of the American Bar Association and a Committee of Publishers and Associations.

The information provided herein is stated to be truthful and consistent, in that any liability, in terms of inattention or otherwise, by any usage or abuse of any policies, processes, or directions contained within is the solitary and utter responsibility of the recipient reader. Under no circumstances will any legal responsibility or blame be held against the publisher for any reparation, damages, or

# Table of Contents

# Chapter 1: Programming Languages 101

There are three main categories of computer programming language:

## Machine Language

This is the default computer language that is built-in primitive instructions represented to the computer in binary code. Thus, if you want to instruct a computer, you must write in binary code. Here is an example of 'hello world' in binary:

```
01001000 01100101 01101100 01101100 01101111
00100000 01110111 01101111 01110010 01101100
01100100
```

## Assembly Language

Assembly languages are alternatives to machine languages. They use mnemonics to represent machine language instructions. Since computers cannot understand assembly language, we use a program called an assembler to convert assembly language code into machine language code. Compared to machine languages, assembly languages are relatively easier to learn and use but they are still tedious because they are closer to machine language.

## High-Level Programming Languages

The late 1990s ushered in the development of a new generation of computer programming languages called high-level programming languages.

High-level programming languages are English-like computer programming languages that are platform independent, which means code written in high-level programming language can run on any machine or computer.

Almost every programming language in use in the modern programming world is high-level. These languages use statements to instruct a computer to perform sets of instructions. Here is an example of calculating the sum of two numbers using modern programming languages:

```
Number1 = 10

Number2 = 100

Sum = Number1 + Number2
```

Today, we have many high-level programming languages. The list below shows the most popular programming languages, the ones commonly applicable in any field.

- Python

- Java

- C++

- JavaScript

- Ruby

In this guide, we shall be discussing the essentials you need, to master to start programming or writing computer code in three programming languages: Java, C++, and Python (version 3).

The next section starts the discussion by looking at the basic elements whose understanding of which will allow you to get started on the path to being a proficient programmer.

# Chapter 2: Programming Basics

Like human languages, high-level programming languages have a set of key elements. Most high-level programming languages have the following core elements:

- Environments

- Keywords

- Data Types

- Variables

- Operators

- Control Flow

- Functions

- Arrays

- Strings

- Inputs/Outputs

In the following chapters, we are going to discuss each element using examples of the three programming languages we mentioned earlier: Java, C++, and Python.

# Environment Setup

Since computers lack the ability to understand high-level programming languages directly, we us a translator or convertor where we write our code and then translate it to machine code. We call this a development environment.

Although not a programming element by itself, setting up your development environment is usually the very first step to working with every programming language. It mainly comprises of installing a certain type of software on your computer so that you can create computer code and translate this code into language your computer can understand.

With most high-level programming languages, the most notable tools necessary to create a conventional programming environment are:

## 1: Text Editor

A text editor is a piece of software we use to write computer code in plain text without formatting. Microsoft Windows has Notepad as its default text editor. Source code is the name we use to refer to Code written and saved by text editor.

## 2: Translators

We use translators to convert source code into binary language. The binary code translated then becomes what programmers refer to as 'object code.' Translators can be:

1. **Assemblers:** We use these to convert low-level languages into machine code.

2. **Compilers:** Compilers convert source code to binary code and then execute the binary. If the program runs into an error during the execution process, the compilation stops without creating a binary. The most popular compiled languages are C, C++, Objective-C, Swift, and Pascal.

3. **Interpreters:** Interpreters are similar to compilers but instead of running the entire program, they convert the code line by line. This means that every line of code runs until an error occurs. Once the program returns an error, the interpreter automatically stops and reports the error. The most popular interpreted languages are Python, Ruby, JavaScript, and Perl.

4. **Hybrid Translators:** Hybrid translators are a combination of compilers and interpreters. They convert the source code into Bytecode. Runtime engines then

translate and execute the bytecode. The main example here is Java that uses the Java Virtual Machine (JVM).

**NOTE:** Set up your programming environment depending on the various instructions given by each of the three programming languages we shall be working with—and each language has different environment setup instructions.

As mentioned earlier, in this guide, we shall be using Java, C++, and Python to illustrate the ten basic elements mentioned earlier. We shall primarily use Java for illustrations. Use the following resource pages to learn how to install the pieces of software you need to have installed on your computer to start writing computer code in the Java programming language:

https://www.tutorialspoint.com/java/java_environment_setup

https://www.wikihow.com/Set-Up-a-Java-Programming-Environment

https://www.youtube.com/watch?v=kh_3Eoy9obE

# Chapter 3: Getting Started

The very first computer program we are going to write prints a string of text on the computer screen.

As mentioned in the closing sections of the last chapter, all hands-on tutorials found in this guide will be using Java to illustrate how to program or create computer code. With that mentioned, note that we shall also provide examples using the other two programming languages mentioned earlier (C++ and Python).

Start up your programming environment and type the following computer code exactly as shown:

```java
public class Main
{
    public static void main(String[] args) {
        System.out.println("Hello World");
    }
}
```

If you run the code above, it prints the string 'Hello World' on the computer screen.

# First Program: Hello World

In a Java program, the first piece of code is the **class name** of the program. We will now concentrate on breaking down the details of how each statement works.

First, the **public** keyword is an Access Identifier that specifies how the method or class will be accessible. The public keyword makes the class accessible globally. The next keyword is **class**. In the java programming language, we use this keyword to define a new class.

The next keyword is **main**. The Main string is an identifier of the class name. In Java, we indicate the definition of a class by the starting and end of curly braces {}.

The second line of the statement represents the main method in a java program. Every Java program must contain the main method. The **static** keyword helps the Virtual Machine—JVM—load the class into memory and execute the main method; if the static keyword is missing, Java Virtual Machine (JVM) will return an error. The **void** keyword tells the JVM that the method does not have a return type. The **main** is the name of the main method. The **string[] args**, the Java main method, accepts only one argument of type String as an array.

The third line statement has a unique statement. **System** represents the final class in the java.lang packages. **Out** represents a class variable declared in the System class. **Println** is a method in the PrintStream class.

## Hello World in Python

You can write the above hello world program in many programming languages, including Python. The following code will print 'Hello World' in python:

```python
print('Hello World')
```

## Hello World in C++

To write a C++ program that prints a Hello World statement on the screen, we write the following C++ computer code:

```cpp
#include <iostream>
int main()
{
    std::cout << << std::endl; << "Hello, World!";
    return 0;
}
```

Now that you have seen how easy it actually is to start writing programs using different programming languages, the next chapter is going to give you a firm understanding of the ten, core elements you are likely to work with irrespective of which programming language you chose to work with or master.

# Chapter 4: Master These Programming Elements

This chapter is the most valuable in the book. From it, you are going to learn how to work with the aforementioned core elements found in most high-level programming languages:

## How to Work with Keywords

In programming languages, "keywords" refers to the defined syntax that reserves specific words as its own. For example, in English, the word 'his' is a pronoun that you cannot use as a Noun.

Since each programming language has its own defined syntax, we cannot exhaustively discuss all the keywords used by every programming language. Instead, what we are going to do is look at commonly reserved keywords in most programming languages:

The Java programming language provides the following keywords

| final | return | double | float | continue | short |
|-------|--------|--------|-------|----------|-------|
| if | finally | const | try | default | switch |
| else | new | break | this | long | extends |
| int | throw | char | for | private | do |
| class | void | import | while | public | catch |

**NOTE:** This is but a sampling of some of the common Java Keywords. For all reserved keywords, check out java documentation:

For python, here are the most common keywords:

| pass | continue | with | else | raise | elif |
|------|----------|------|------|-------|------|
| def | finally | is | try | global | assert |
| from | del | in | except | False | break |
| and | __init__ | class | for | exec | default |
| import | lambda | print | while | if | True |

Keywords reserved for C++ programming language include:

| int | for | goto | switch | Class | catch |
|-----|-----|------|--------|-------|-------|
| const | continue | short | if | public | char |
| return | float | default | for | private | template |
| void | double | register | while | Try | Using |
| volatile | do | else | struct | throw | namespace |

**NOTE:** You do not have to memorize each language's keywords. The sole reason for pointing out these keywords is so that you can take note and be mindful or careful not to use these reserved keywords as variable names.

## How to Work with Data Types

Most popular programming languages have an important element called data types. Data types are representation of types of data processed by the computer in a program.

For this section, we are going to use examples to explain core concepts:

### Example 1:

100 + 100 = 200

$200 - 10 = 190$

$5 * 34 = 170$

$200 / 33 = 6.06061$

## **Example 2:**

Name: 'Susan Jean'

Division: 'B'

The above examples show different types of data common in most programming languages. The first example shows data type of numbers such as integers and floats. The second example shows strings and characters. When writing computer programs, we must define the type of data we want to use.

Although some languages do not explicitly require you to define the type of data, most languages require it so; otherwise, the program returns an error and does not know the type of operations you want carried out on the data.

Let us break down the data types in the above examples

- 100, 200 and other whole numbers are integers (int)

- 6.06061 and other decimal numbers are floating numbers (floats)

- Susan, Jean, and other sequence of characters are strings (str)

- B and single characters are characters (char)

Those are some of the common data types across programming languages. C++, C, and Java may share common data types with Java providing additional Data types.

Here is a table of C++ data types:

| char | Single characters |
|---|---|
| int | Whole numbers, integers |
| float | Single precision floating numbers |
| double | Double precision floating numbers |
| bool | Boolean values |
| struct | Grouped data |

For Java, the data types are similar to the ones above.

Python has five typical data types. However, python does not require the data type keyword before using the data; because it is intelligent enough, it knows the data type automatically. Atypical data types in Python include:

- Numbers – integers, floats complex

- Strings

- Booleans

- Lists

- Tuple

- Dictionaries

# How to Work with Variables

In programming, the term 'variable' refers to a storage location in the computer memory; we use variables to store information for retrieval, reference, and manipulation within a computer program.

For example, if you want to capture the name of a user, you will need to store it in the computer under a specific name. Creating or declaring a variable is one of the most difficult tasks in programming; this is because it requires creative naming structures that do not use reserved keywords and that follow the rules of naming a variable.

In Java, we declare a variable as follows:

```java
public class Main
{
    public static void main(String[] args) {
        int firstArgument;
        double secondArgument;

        firstArgument = 100;
        secondArgument = 125.50;

        // now you can referrence the values
        System.out.println('The value of firstArgument is' +firstArgument);
        System.out.println('The value of secondArgument is' +secondArgument);
    }
}
```

The above program has two variables: firstArgument and secondArgument of the type integer and double respectively.

The program then allocates their values as 100 and 125.50 according to their type of data. The program then references the variables using their names and then prints them on the screen.

In C++, we declare variable as follows:

```cpp
#include <iostream>
using namespace std;

int main() {
    int number1, number2, sum;

    number1 = 100;
    number2 = 120;

    sum = number1 + number2;

    cout << number1 << endl;
    cout << number2 << endl;

    cout << "The sum of the two number is" << sum << endl;

    return 0;
}
```

The above C++ program creates three variables and reserved memory locations namely number1, number2, and sum. As you can see, we defined the data type before using the variables. We then accessed the variables stored in the memory using their names.

Python variable declaration is as illustrated below:

```python
x = 10
y = 10.5
name = 'John'

print('X is: ', x)
print('Y is: ', y)
print(name, 'set the sum as', x+y)
```

As you can see, python is very flexible and does not require you to specify the data type before using the data. This makes python very vast and fast-to-use when creating large computations and programs.

## How to Work with Operators

In programming, we use operators to perform specific operation on a data type to generate new results. Here, we are only going to discuss the following types of operators:

- Arithmetic Operators

- Relational Operators

- Logical Operators

# 1: Arithmetic Operators

In programming, we use arithmetic operators for basic mathematical operations. They perform calculations on supported data types. We can write computer programs that perform arithmetic operations such as adding two or more numbers together.

## Example:

101 + 102 = 202

100 - 10 = 90

The above statements are what we call arithmetic statements as they use arithmetic operators. Most programming language have arithmetic operators specific to them.

The following table shows arithmetic operators for Java:

| + | Additional Operator | 10 + 10 = 20 |
|---|---|---|
| - | Subtraction Operator | 100 − 45 = 55 |
| * | Multiplication operator | 40 * 40 = 1600 |
| / | Division Operator | 166 / 33 = 5.0303 |
| % | Modulo Operator | 10 % 3 = 1 |

Arithmetic operators are similar across many languages. However, other languages provide additional operators. Python adds the exponent (**) operator.

The following figure shows arithmetic operations using java:

```java
public class Main
{
    public static void main(String[] args) {

        int i = 73;
        int j = 32;
        double x = 26.475;
        double y = 18.22;

        System.out.println("i + j: " + i + j);
        System.out.println("x - y: " + y - x);
        System.out.println("i x j: " + i * j);
        System.out.println("x / y: " + x / y);
        System.out.println("i % j: " + i % j);

    }
}
```

Arithmetic operators in C++ are similar to Java as long as the data type supports the type of operations. All the three languages we are using for illustration purposes support String concatenation, addition of strings together to form one string.

```python
print(10 + 10) # 20
print(100 - 30) # 70
print(50 * 16) # 800
print(90 / 7) # 12.857142857142858
print(40 % 12) # 4
print(10**3) # = 1000
name = 'Python'

print(name + ' is awesome') # Python is awesome
```

## 2: Relational Operators

In computer programming, we use Relational operators to perform comparison operators among data types. An example would be to check whether a number is greater than or less than a certain value. For example,

A = 10

B = 100

A > B

The above operator (>) checks whether the value A is greater than value B. These types of operators are what we call relational operators. The result of these types of operation is either True or False, which is a Boolean value. They are common among all programming languages. The table below shows relational operators in all languages.

| > | Greater than |
|---|---|
| < | Less than operator |
| >= | Greater than or equal to |
| <= | Less than or equal to |
| != | Not equal to |
| == | Equal to |

The following is an example of using Java and relational operators.

```java
public class Main {

    public static void main(String[] args) {
        int num1 = 16, num2 = 8;
        System.out.println("num1 == num2 = " + (num1 == num2) ); // false
        System.out.println("num1 != num2 = " + (num1 != num2) ); // true
        System.out.println("num1 >  num2 = " + (num1 >  num2) ); // true
        System.out.println("num1 <  num2 = " + (num1 <  num2) ); // false
        System.out.println("num1 >= num2 = " + (num1 >= num2) ); // true
        System.out.println("num1 <= num2 = " + (num1 <= num2) ); // false
    }
}
```

These operators are similar across Java, C++, and Python and it is therefore not necessary to give examples for the individual programming languages we are working with here.

### 3: Logical Operators

Logical operators, also called Boolean operators in programming, are very important. We use them to make decisions based on the conditions returned. We normally use them in combination with arithmetic and relational operators.

Suppose we want to compare two different conditions, we can do this using the logical operators. Operationally, Logical operators are similar across all programming languages but they can be different on a syntax level.

The following table shows basic logical operators for Java and C++.

| | |
|---|---|
| ! | Logical NOT – returns true if the condition evaluates to false |
| && | Logical AND – returns true if both conditions evaluate to true. |
| \|\| | Logical OR – returns true if one of the conditions is true. |

Both Java and C++ provide identical logical statements. For python, the logical operators are similar except we write them in text as illustrated in the table below:

| Operator | Description |
|---|---|
| and | Logical AND – returns true if both conditions evaluate to true. |
| or | Logical OR – returns true if one of the conditions evaluate to true |
| not | Logical Not – Used to reverse the overall condition. Returns true if the condition is false. |

# How to Work with Control Flow

Control flow is perhaps the most important element in programming. This is because Control flow allows us to make decisions and perform certain operations in a given condition. Control flow has two different aspects.

- Selection Statements

- Iteration Statements

Let us discuss these types of control flow statements for the languages we are working with.

## 1: Selection Statements

In coding, you may encounter a situation where you need to perform certain conditional checks. A good example is if you were to grade something based on its weight.

Almost all programming languages provide a universal selection conditional check. The following illustration shows the logic behind selection statements for all languages.

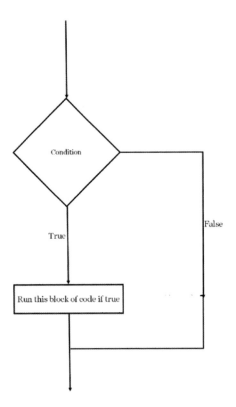

Let us write a program to illustrate the following code using Java. Use your Java programming environment to write the following code:

```java
public class Main
{
    public static void main(String[] args) {
        int score = 80;
        if (score >= 60) {
            System.out.println('Failed');
        }
        if(score >= 70) {
            System.out.println("Average");
        }
        if (score >= 80) {
            System.out.println("Passed")
        }
    }
}
```

We can also write a C++ program as follows.

```cpp
#include <iostream>
using namespace std;
int main() {
    int x = 50;
    if( x > 95) {

        cout << "Student is brilliant" << endl;
    }
    if( x < 30) {
        cout << "Student is poor" << endl;
    }
    if( x < 95 && x > 30 ) {
        cout << "Student is average" << endl;
    }
    return 0;
}
```

For python, the case is as shown below:

```python
age = 18

if (age > 18):
    print('Allowed')
if (age < 18):
    print('Not Allowed')
```

All the above examples illustrate use of 'if statements' to check conditions and perform particular operations if certain conditions are true. You can chain if statements to an else statement to check multiple conditions. The syntax for if...else if...else statement for Java and C++ is

```
if(boolean_condition 1) {

}

else if( boolean_condition 2) {

}

else if( boolean_condition 3) {

} else {

}
```

For python, the same case applies except the else...if statement uses the elif statement.

## 2: Iteration Statements

Iteration statements, also called loops, are statements used to run a certain condition a number of times repeatedly as long as a condition evaluates to true. Suppose we want to print the string 'Hello World' 10 times, we can use a loop to accomplish this task. Almost all programming languages have looping capabilities.

## While Loop

In most programming languages, the while loop performs certain operations as long as a specific condition remains true. The following example shows usage of while loop in Java.

```java
public class Main {
    public static void main(String []args) {
        int i = 0;

        while ( i < 5 ) {
            System.out.println("Hello, World!");
            i = i + 1;
        }
    }
}
```

The above program prints the string 'Hello world' five times as the condition. The code to run while the condition is true is under the curly braces. The while loop is modifiable using two keywords: break and continue statements.

- **Break:** When encountered in a loop, the break statement stops the execution and jumps to the next block of code.

- **Continue:** The continue statement works the same way as a break statement does but instead of forcing termination of the execution, it forces the condition to continue the loop.

Python and C++ support while loops with break and continue statements.

## do...while

A do...while loop is similar to a while loop but has a slight difference. In a while loop, the program first checks the condition before executing the statement in the loop body.

On the other hand, the do...while loop executes the statement within it then checks the condition. Only Java and C++ support do...while loops—python does not. The syntax for do...while loop is as follows and is similar in Java and C++:

```cpp
#include <iostream>
using namespace std;
int main(){
    int num=2;
    do{
        cout<<"Value of num: "<<num<<endl;
        num++;
    }while(num<=7);
    return 0;
}
```

## For Loop

For loop is the most common type of loop in programming. By design, it iterates through a number of specified times. The for loop is first initialized, conditioned, and then incremented or decremented accordingly. The following is an example of a Java for loop.

```java
public class Main {
public static void main(String[] args) {

    for(int i=1;i<=10;i++){
        System.out.println(i);
    }
}
}
```

When you run the above program, it will display all the numbers from 1 to 10. A for loop is also available in python. Here is an example of a for loop in python.

```python
numbers = [1, 2, 4, 6, 11, 20]
square = 0
for val in numbers:
    square = val * val
    print(square)
```

Make sure your loop condition finally evaluates to false or it will never end. A loop that does not end creates an infinite loop.

# How to Work with Functions/Methods

A function or method is a block of reusable code organized to perform one or multiple operations. Some programming languages call functions methods—this is specific to Java—or sub-routines and procedures in other languages. We shall use the term function to refer to both terms.

Functions allow the highest degree of code reusability and modularity. We have already seen some common functions such as println() in java, main() in C++, and print() in python.

When creating a function, the first step is declaration. Declaration of functions/methods can vary between languages. Here, we are going to work with functions in all three languages: Java, C++, and Python.

## Methods in Java

Let us see how to create a function in Java. The simple syntax for creating a Java method is below:

```
modifier returnType methodName(parameters) {

        Method body

}
```

```
public static double myMethod(double 1, double b) {
    // method body goes here
}
```

The above method contains a modifier, a return type, and method name. A detailed working of a Java method is as follows:

- **Modifier:** This specifies the return type of access the method contains. It could be public, private, static, and more. The modifier part of a Java function is optional.

- **Return Type:** This specifies the type of value returned from the method. Some methods do not have a return type thus set to void.

- **Name of method:** This is the name of the method. You can name it whatever you want so long as the name makes sense and does not conflict with rules of naming.

- **Parameters:** This contains the arguments the method can accept. This part of the method declaration is also optional since not all methods require parameters.

- **Body:** This contains the block of code that the method performs.

Below is a Java method that checks and returns the maximum number of two values.

```java
public class Main
{
    public static void main(String[] args) {
        int a = 10;
        int b = 3;
        int c = max(a, b);

        System.out.println(c);
    }
    public static int max(arg1, arg2) {
        int temp;

        if (arg1 > arg2) {
            temp = arg1;|
        }
        else {
            temp = arg2;
        }
    }
}
```

After declaring a method, you use it by calling it using its name and providing its arguments where required. If the called method returns a value, the value passes to the caller.

**NOTE:** In Java and C++, we use the keyword void to define methods that do not return a value.

## Functions in C++

In C++, Functions works the same way as Java methods. When you declare a C++ function, it tells the compiler the function name, its arguments, and the return type of the function. Let us look at ways to declare a C++ functions.

The syntax is similar to that of Java.

```
returnType functionName (Arguments) {

        function body

}
```

Similar to Java Methods, the return type, function name, and arguments perform similar operations. The image below shows the Java max() Method in C++

```cpp
#include <iostream>
using namespace std;
int max(int arg1, int arg2) {
    int temp;

    if (arg1 > arg2)
        temp = arg1;
    else
        temp = arg2;

    return temp;
}
int main() {
    int arg1 = 100;
    int arg2 = 50;
    int result = max(arg1, arg2);

    cout << result << endl;
    return 0;
}
```

Similar to the Java method, when calling C++ function, you use its name and pass the required parameters.

## Function in Python

Python also works well with functions; it actually has the simplest function declaration. However, when it comes to declaring functions, python follows some rules. The most important of these rules are:

- We declare Function using the def keyword followed by the function name.

- Arguments of a python function should be within parenthesis.

- Always close the parenthesis with colons.

- Always indent the function body inside the function declaration.

The syntax for declaring the python function is as follows:

```
def myFunction(arguments):

        // should be indented
```

The same operation of calling a python function is similar to that of Java and C++. The example below shows the same max function in python.

```python
def max(a, b):
    temp = 0
    if (a > b):
        temp = a
    else:
        temp = b
    return temp


result = max(10, 20)
print(result)
```

We have covered the basics of functions and methods using three main programming languages. We are now going to cover another programming element known as arrays.

# How to Work with Arrays

An array is a data container that stores a collection of elements with indexes. In some programming languages such as python, arrays are 'Lists.' Although there are noticeable array operations differences across programming languages, arrays or lists perform similarly across different programming languages.

We are going to discuss how to work with array using the three programming languages we have discussed thus far:

## Arrays in Java

Suppose you wanted to store integers from 1 to 100, you would start to declare variables such as int num1, int num2, int num3...int num100. Writing the above program code would be hectic and very repetitive. This is where arrays come in hand.

To declare an array in Java, we use the new keyword. The syntax is as shown below:

```
datatype[] arrayReferenceValue ;
```

To create an array, we use the **new** keyword in java followed by the data type of array we want to create and the length of the array elements. The following example shows how to create an array called myArray of type double and the length.

```java
public class Main
{
    public static void main(String[] args) {
        double[] myArray = new double[100];
    }
}
```

Once you create an array, you can perform operations on the array. Let us see how to access elements in array in Java.

You can access the elements in an array by passing the index of the element. The array indexing in Java starts at index 0. For example:

```java
public class Main
{
    public static void main(String[] args) {
        double[] myList = {1.9, 2.9, 3.4, 3.5};
        double name = myList[0];
        System.out.println(name);
    }
}
```

Once the above program runs, it returns the value 1.9. To access the value 2.9, you pass the index as 1.

## Arrays in C++

Just like Java and other high-level programming, C++ provides the ability to store values in an array. To create an array in C++, you need to provide the type of elements and the number of elements to store in the array.

The syntax is as follows:

```
type arrayName [size_of_Array]
```

An array of this type is what we call a single-dimensional array. We are only going to look at single-dimensional arrays. To initialize an array in C++, you just pass the elements in the array. The elements in the array cannot exceed the length of the array you declared. Similar to Java arrays, when accessing the elements in array, you just pass the index of the element you want to access.

For example:

```cpp
#include <iostream>
using namespace std;
int main()
{
    double myArray[5] = {100, 200, 300, 500, 600};
    // to access a value in the array
    int myBal = myArray[4]; // returns 600
    return 0;
}
```

**NOTE:** Java supports C++ way of array creation but we do not recommend using this method.

## Python Lists

Python lists are not necessarily similar to Java and C++ arrays but are close enough. Python is so flexible that Lists support different kinds of data, which is novel because in most programming languages, arrays can only contain one type of data. For example, if you create an array of integers, the elements within it must be integers only. For python, the case is different.

To create a python list, just pass the name of the list followed by square brackets and the name elements within the list. For example:

```
myList = [100, 'peter', [100,200,300],'Jane','Charlotte']
# list in python can contain integers, floats, strings and even list with it
```

Python arrays are very flexible and are a very important data structure within Python. Do not confuse python Lists with Dictionaries.

**NOTE:** This book does not discuss Python dictionaries. You can access the elements in an array similar to Java and C++. Python uses zero indexing meaning the first element in a list is index 0.

## How to Work with Strings

Strings are very important elements in programming. In some languages such as C—though not discussed in this guide—data types such as strings are not available by default. In other words, C only supports characters and represents a string (which is more than one character) as an array of characters.

Java and other advanced programming languages provide string as a data type. This means you can define strings on their own without allocating them as an array of single characters. To create a string in Java, you define the data type as a string then the variable name.

```java
public class Main
{
    public static void main(String[] args) {
        String myName = "Hello";
        System.out.println(myName);
    }
}
```

C++ is a more improved version of C with Object-Oriented Programming support and more advanced functionality. C++ supports the creation of strings using an array of characters. However, C++ provides the string type that allows direct creation of strings. The figure below shows the creation of strings using C++

```cpp
#include <iostream>
#include <string>
using namespace std;

int main () {

    string str1 = "Hello";
    string str2 = "World ";
    cout << str1 + str2 << endl;
}
```

To create a string in python, you just name the variable and then set the value of the string as illustrated below:

```python
myString = 'Hello World'
print(myString)
```

# How to Work with Inputs & Outputs

Here, we are going to learn how to create programs that interact with the user. So far, we have only seen how to print information from the user. If we want to accept input from the user's keyboard, we must use in-built functions within our programming language.

To accept input from Java, we must first import some packages. Java uses the System.out to print information on the screen. For input, we use the System.in, which you must import before use. The procedure is as illustrated below:

```java
import java.util.Scanner;
public class Main
{
    Scanner input = new Scanner(System.in); //creates object of Scanner type
    public static void main(String[] args) {
        System.out.println("Enter a number: ");
        int number = input.nextInt();
    }
}
```

In Java, we do the imports before the main class definition.

To accept input from the user in C++, we use the cin method provided for use. The code below is an example:

```cpp
#include <iostream>
using namespace std;
int main()
{
    double distance;
    cout << "Enter the distance: " << endl;
    cin >> distance;
    cout << distance << endl;
}
```

In python, input is very easy. We use the input function provided by python. The difference in python is that all input is a string data type that you need to convert to the desired data type.

```python
name = input("Enter your name: ")
print(name)
```

For example, if you want to calculate the age of a user based on the year of birth, you must convert the provided year into an integer from a string. Let us perform this operation without converting it to a number. Type the following code and run it:

```
1  import datetime
2  YOB = input("Enter your year birth: ")
3  now = datetime.datetime.now()
4
5  age = now.year - YOB
6  print(age)
```

```
Enter your year birth: 1998
Traceback (most recent call last):
  File "main.py", line 5, in <module>
    age = now.year - YOB
TypeError: unsupported operand type(s) for -: 'int' and 'str'
```

Python returns **a TypeError** saying you cannot perform arithmetic operation between an integer data type and string data type. To fix the error, you must convert the YOB to integer as follows.

```
1  import datetime
2  YOB = int(input("Enter your year birth: "))
3  now = datetime.datetime.now()
4  age = now.year - YOB
5  print(age)
```

```
Enter your year birth: 1998
21
```

This chapter has covered every element you need to master to learn programming in the three most widely used languages: Java, C++, and Python.

With all programming languages, practice makes perfect; therefore, practice working with these elements using different programming languages. By mastering these elements, you can learn various programming languages fast.

# Chapter 5: Practice Exercises

This chapter has a series of programming exercises meant to help you sharpen the skills learned from this guide.

## Exercise 1

Write a program that accepts the temperature as a double and convert it to Fahrenheit, and display the result. Use C++ and Python to perform this task). The formula for conversion is:

$$°F = \left(\frac{9}{5}\right) * °C + 32$$

A solution in java is below:

```java
import java.util.Scanner;
public class Main
{
    public static void main(String[] args) {
        Scanner input = new Scanner(System.in);
        System.out.println("Enter the temp in celcius:");  // make sure to pass the value as double
        double temp = input.nextDouble();
        double tempFah = (temp * 9/5) + 32;
        System.out.println(temp+ " celcius is " +tempFah+ " in Fahrenheit");
    }
}
```

## Exercise 2

Calculate runaway length.

Using Python, calculate the minimum length of a runaway given the plane's acceleration and take-off speed. Use the formula $L = \frac{v2}{2a}$ where a = take-off speed and v is the acceleration.

A solution in Java is below:

```java
import java.util.Scanner;
public class Main
{
    public static void main(String[] args) {
        Scanner input = new Scanner(System.in);
        System.out.println("Enter the take of speed in as double: ");
        double take_off_speed = input.nextDouble();
        System.out.println("Enter the accelaration: ");
        double acceleration = input.nextDouble();
        double min_runaway = (acceleration * acceleration) / (2 * take_off_speed);
        System.out.println("The minimum runaway required is: " +min_runaway);
    }
}
```

## Exercise 3

Using Zeller's congruence algorithm, write a program that calculates the day of the week. Use any of the three languages discussed in this guide. The formula for the algorithm is:

$$h = \left( q + \frac{26(m+1)}{10} + k + \frac{k}{4} + \frac{j}{4} + 5j \right) \% 7$$

- H = the day of the week

- q = day of the month

- m = the month

- j = the century

- k = the year of the century

More information on Zeller's algorithm is available here.

https://en.wikipedia.org/wiki/Zeller%27s_congruence

Here is solution of the algorithm written in C++

```cpp
// zeller algorithim in c++
# include <iostream>
# include <cmath>
# include <cstring>
using namespace std;
int algorithim(int day, int month,
          int year)
{
if (month == 1)
{
   month = 13;
   year--;
}
if (month == 2)
{
   month = 14;
   year--;
}
int q = day;
int m = month;
int k = year % 100;
int j = year / 100;
int h = q + 13*(m+1)/5 + k + k/4 + j/4 + 5*j;
h = h % 7;
switch (h)
{
   case 0 : cout << "Saturday \n"; break;
   case 1 : cout << "Sunday \n"; break; |
   case 2 : cout << "Monday \n"; break;
   case 3 : cout << "Tuesday \n"; break;
   case 4 : cout << "Wednesday \n"; break;
   case 5 : cout << "Thursday \n"; break;
   case 6 : cout << "Friday \n"; break;
}
return 0;
}
int main()
{
algorithim(6, 8, 2019); //date (dd/mm/yyyy)
return 0;
}
```

## Exercise 4

Using any of the three programming languages we have discussed, write a loop to display the following letter pattern (Use a for loop)

```
                1

            1 2 1

          1 2 4 21

        1 2 4 8 4 2 1

      1 2 4 8 16 8 4 2 1

    1   2 4 8 16 32 16 8 4 2 1

   1 2 4 8 16 32 64 32 16 8 4 2 1

 1 2 4 8 16 32 64 128 64 32 16 8 4 2 1
```

## Exercise 5

Using Java, write a method with this header (public static int pentNumber(int num) to return a pentagonal number. You can learn more about pentagonal numbers from the following resource page:

https://en.wikipedia.org/wiki/Pentagonal_number

## Exercise 6

Using the internet, download a text-editor, a C++ compiler and setup your programming environment according to your operating system. Download and Install Java and Python.

Use the following links for official and trusted downloads:

https://www.python.org/downloads/

https://www.oracle.com/technetwork/java/javase/downloads/jdk8-downloads-2133151.html

## Exercise 7

Using C++ and Java only, write a program that computes the energy essential to heat a liquid from initial temperature to final temperature. The program should accept the weight of the liquid from in kg, initial temp, and final temp. The formula for energy calculation is $Q = W * (Final - Initial) * 4184$ where W is the weight of the liquid.

# Conclusion

Thank you again for purchasing this book!

As you have seen, learning how to program and write code is fun and easy enough provided you master the ten basic elements discussed in this guide.

Keep in mind that being a coder or programmer is a skill; the more you practice by writing computer code and programs, the faster your skills will grow.

Finally, if you enjoyed this book, would you be kind enough to leave a review for this book on Amazon?

https://www.amazon.com/dp/B07WLS3CNM

Thank you and good luck!

Printed in Great Britain
by Amazon

54955674R00035